누가, 앉아 있다

고요아침 운문정신 014

누가, 앉아 있다
Someone Is Sitting

김민정 수석壽石 시조집

Min-Jung Kim's Collection
of Sijo Poems about Viewing Stones

김민정 지음
우형숙 번역

Written by Min-Jung Kim
Translated by Hyung-Sook Woo

고요아침

| 시인의 말 |

  몇 해 전부터 돌과 가까운 시간을 가졌다. 이 어줍은 연애. 그저 좋아서 강과 바다를 다니며 더운 줄도 추운 줄도 모르고 설레며 헤맨 날들…
  수석은 한자로 수석壽石 또는 수석水石이라고도 표기하는데, 예로부터 자연을 사랑하는 선비들에게 친근한 벗이었다. 수석은 산지에 따라 흙에서 나는 돌土中石, 강에서 나는 돌江石, 바다에서 나는 돌海石로 나뉜다. 또 색채석, 문양석, 산수경석, 물형석, 변화석, 추상석, 인상석 등 다양하게 나누기도 한다.
  월간《수석문화》와《나래시조》에 수석시를 연재한 지도 3년이 되어간다. 그 결과 수석인은 시조를, 시조시인은 수석을 이해하는 계기가 되었다는 것에 뿌듯함을 느낀다.
  혹자는 수석시가 시조의 폭을 좁힌다고도 하고, 혹자는 시조가 수석에 대한 상상력을 좁힌다고도 한다. 그러나 나는 그 반대로 생각하고 싶다. 수석에는 삼라만상의 모습이 들어 있으니 그에 대한 시조를 씀으로써 수석은 가치를 더해 가고, 시조는 구체적인 이미지로 독자들과 가까워진다는 생각이다.

이 시집에 실린 수석들은 거의 문양석이며, 몇 개만 형상석이다. 수석 전문가들에게 인정받은 명석도 있고, 내 품에 안겨 나만의 명석이 된 것도 있음을 밝힌다.

이번에 60편을 선별하여 영어번역을 곁들여 수석시조집을 발간한다. 모쪼록 많은 분들의 사랑받는 시집이었으면 하는 바람, 간절하다.

찾기란 쉽지 않다
어둠 뚫는 한 줄기 빛

멋스런 질감, 색감
공감하는 문양까지

골고루
모양새 갖춘
너를 직접 만나기란
—「수석」 전문

2017년 8월
김민정

| Preface |

I have had a close relationship with stones since some years ago. It's an awkward love. I have just enjoyed going around rivers and seas with expectation regardless of hot weather and cold weather.

A viewing stone is written as 壽石 or 水石 in Chinese, and it has been a close friend to scholars since ancient times. According to a place of origin, viewing stones are divided into three kinds: ground stones, river stones, and sea stones. What's more, they can be divided into the following: color stones, figure stones, landscape stones, object stones, altered stones, abstract stones, human-face stones, etc.

It's been three years since I wrote Sijo poems about viewing stones for the monthly viewing stone magazine *Suseok munhwa* and the literary magazine *Narae Sijo*. It was a good chance to make viewing stone collectors understand Sijo and to make Sijo writers know about viewing stones. Now I feel gratified.

Some say that viewing stone Sijo poems narrow the range of Sijo poems, and others say that Sijo poems narrow their imagination about viewing stones. But

I think of it from a different angle. As viewing stones contain all things in nature, writing Sijo poems about the stones can enhance the value of viewing stones, and Sijo poems can get near Sijo readers with concrete images.

The stones in this collection are almost figure stones, and some others are shape stones. Among my stones, some earned good recognition from stone experts, and others became my own precious stones in my bosom.

Now my collection of 60 Sijo poems about viewing stones is published, along with the translation into English. It's my highest aspiration that this collection will gain me a wide audience with great love.

It's like a light through the dark;
it's not easy to find you,

who have agreeable figures,
fancy textures and good colors.

In person
to meet you, who have
diverse shapes, isn't easy.
— *A Viewing Stone*

August, 2017
Min-Jung Kim

| 차례 |

시인의 말 Preface　　　　　　　　　　　　　　04

제1부/ 봄의 탄주彈奏 A Spring Performance

봄의 탄주彈奏 A Spring Performance　　　　　　15
거북의 길 The Turtle's Way　　　　　　　　　19
금강산에서 On Mt. Keumkang　　　　　　　　23
낙타 A Camel　　　　　　　　　　　　　　　27
누가, 앉아 있다 Someone Is Sitting　　　　　　31
오세암 이야기 A Story of Oseam Temple　　　　35
사랑 앞에 In Front of Love　　　　　　　　　39
심포리 기찻길 Shimpori Railroad　　　　　　　43
선덕의 외출 Queen Seondeok's Outing　　　　　47
아침, 정동진 The Morning of Jeongdongjin　　　51
부표를 읽다 Reading the Buoy　　　　　　　　55
안개에 젖어 Being Wet in the Mist　　　　　　59
모래울음을 찾아 In Search of the Sand Crying　63

제2부/ 꽃밤 The Flowering Night

꽃밤 The Flowering Night	69
농악놀이 The Play of a Farm Band	71
누가 오시나 Who's Gonna Come	73
달밤 A Moonlight Night	75
꽃, 그 순간 A Flower, at the Momentt	77
그리고, 별 And, the Star	79
가을 뎃생 An Autumn Sketch	81
고목 An Aged Tree	83
강론하는 교황님 The Preaching Pope	85
과묵 Reticence	87
난 송이 두엇 A Few Orchid Flowers	89
저 길을 따라서 Along the Way	91

제3부/ 부부 Husband and Wife

부부 Husband and Wife	95
돌꽃, 진달래 Stone Blossoms, Azalea	97
담금질 Tempering	99
둥근 꽃 The Round Flower	101
따스한 입맞춤 A Warm Kiss	103
때때로 Once in a While	105
말문을 닫다 Saying No More	107
매화 향기 바람에 날리고 The Fragrance of Ume Flowers Whirled by the Wind	109
불국토 The Buddha's Land	111
비밀 Secrecy	113
천불동에 무릎 꿇고 Kneeling at Qianfodong	115

제4부/ 웃음 다이어트 A Laughter Diet

웃음 다이어트 A Laughter Diet	119
수양버들 A Willow Tree	121
쉼표 A Comma	123
신화 A Myth	125
십일월 생각 A November Thought	127
어부바 Pickaback	129
어유도魚遊圖 A Fish-playing Painting	131
장독대 A Soy-jar Terrace	133
절규 The Scream	135
주목 앞에서 In Front of a Yew Tree	137
주상절리 A Columnar Joint	139
폭포와 시 The Waterfall and Poems	141

제5부/ 첫눈 오는 날 The Day of the First Snow

첫눈 오는 날 The Day of the First Snow	145
촛대 바위 A Candlestick-shaped Rock	147
풍악산을 건너다 Crossing Mt. Pungak	149
모과 A Quince	151
해빙기 The Thawing Season	153
해수관음보살 The Buddhist Goddess Facing the Sea	155
홍매 Red Apricot Blossoms	157
황산벌에서 At the Hwangsan Plain	159
휘파람 Whistle	161
흑룡이 날으샤 A Black Dragon Flies	165
타클라마칸 사막 The Taklamakan Desert	167
대흥사 부처님께 To Buddha of the Daeheung Temple	171

제 1부

봄의 탄주彈奏

A Spring Performance

「봄의 탄주」 을미도, 33×24×18cm

봄의 탄주彈奏

물방울 하나까지 남김없이 빨아들인
꽃대궁의 물관으로 지나가는 시간들이
부풀어 터질 것 같다 팽팽하게 당겨보면

귓전을 쓸고 가는 마음 저 편 풍경 소리
피안은 바로 여기, 네가 너를 보듬는 곳
묵언에 귀 기울이는 하루가 마냥 깊다

만다라 꽃잎으로 순간이 피고 질 때
발그레 물든 영혼 새 봄이 오고 있다
말갛게 웃다가 잠든 아지랑이 목덜미

A Spring Performance

Time passes through the xylem
   of a flower stalk which sucks in
every drop of water
   thoroughly to the last drop.
The time may swell to burst open
   if it is pulled tightly.

The tinkling of wind-bells
   on the other side reaches my ears.
Nirvana is right here
   where you embrace yourself.
To silence I listen with pricked ears;
   then a day becomes so profound.

When a moment blooms and falls
   as the petals of a mandala*,
a new spring comes again
   as a reddish spirit.
The haze smiles purely and naively
   and sinks into a peaceful sleep.

* mandala : a red heavenly flower

「거북의 길」동해, 29×21×13cm

거북의 길

깊푸른 동해물에 맑게 씻긴 생각 건져
목 빼고 발을 들어 바라보는 그 먼 눈길
파도가 오다가 말고 에두르는 아침이다

신라적 수로 부인 그녀 찾아 나선 걸까
잔치라도 벌일 듯이 입가에 도는 웃음
등 뒤에 업은 자식도 꽃망울로 피고 있다

천지를 오고가는 별무리를 따라가며
창창한 줄무늬로 물길을 짚어가며
발걸음 서둘지 않고 오늘도 너는 간다

The Turtle's Way

Picking up the thoughts washed up
   in the deep blue East Sea,
the turtle looks out over the sea
   with the craned neck on the tip toe.
It's the morn when waves stop coming
   but go back to their own place.

Lady Suro of the Sylla Dynasty
   the turtle might go out to find.
As if it's gonna have a feast
   a smile spreads onto its lips.
The cute kid that's carried on its back
   blooms like a flower bud.

Following myriads of stars
　　across the vast universe,
going along a waterway
　　with some deep blue azure stripes,
the turtle goes on even today
　　but it is in no hurry.

「금강산에서」 풍도, 30×22×17cm

금강산에서

내 속에 숨겨 놓은 피리 하나 꺼내들고
신명나게 불고 싶네 이 언덕에 서고 보니
동해도 만물상 앞에 옷깃을 여미고 있네

물은 같은 물이건만 위아래가 갈라져서
뱃길도 끊어지고 바람도 멈칫대니
흰 구름 서너 장 뜯어 종이배나 접을 거나

금강산 줄기 따라 남녘으로 내려가면
두고 온 고향 산천 품을 열어 반길 텐데
망양대 아무 말 없이 돌 속에 스민 가을

On Mt. Keumkang

Taking out a flute hidden in my mind,
   I hope to play a tune on it
in a merry mood on this hill.
   Here I stand, overlooking
the East Sea straighten itself up
   in front of Manmulsang.

The water is all the same,
   but it divides into up and down.
There has been no boat service
   and the wind is fluky and fickle.
Taking down three or four white clouds,
   I'd rather make a paper boat.

If you go down and down southward
   along a range of Mt. Keumkang,
the mountains and streams of your hometown
   will welcome you with open arms.
The autumn of Mangyangdae
   adheres to the stones in silence.

「낙타」 동해, 14×13×6cm

낙타

겨운 삶 등에 지고 모래밭을 타박이며
얼마나 느린 발길로 너는 걸어 왔을까
시간은 모래바람 속, 온 길이 다 묻힌다

너를 통해 흘러왔을 나의 강을 바라보며
뜨거운 고도 향해 휘파람을 불어가며
혹처럼 굽은 생애가 신기루로 흐른다

오랜 어둠을 깨며 멀어지는 밤 같은
한 생애 푸른 비단을 펼쳐놓은 저 달빛
속눈썹 짙게 젖어든 외로운 등이 휜다

A Camel

With a hard life on your back
   you have trudged on the sands.
How slowly you have walked
   I really want to ask.
Time is in the sandy wind;
   all the paths are buried there.

Looking at my river
   which may have flowed through you,
I go forward, whistling
   toward an ideal land.
My bent life like the hump on your back
   is being led in a mirage.

Breaking a long darkness,
   the night is going away.
All its life the moonlight has spread
   azure silk fabrics in the sky.
Thick and wet are your eyelashes;
   your lonely back gets bent again.

「누가, 앉아 있다」 동해, 7×11.5×6cm

누가, 앉아 있다

돌밭에서 내가 만난 몽돌 속 저 한 사람
고단한 삶 언저리 휴식을 취한 사람
우리들
어머니처럼
아니, 나의 어머니가

깨어지고 엎어지고 상처에 얹힌 딱지
아프고 가려웠을 시간을 견뎌가며
진동과
파장을 건너
닿은 꿈이 있었을까

손발을 쉬지 않고 바쁘게 달려 왔을
장터 어디 쪽의자에 한 생을 내려놓고
뭐라고
말문을 뗄 듯
머뭇대고 있는 사람

Someone Is Sitting

On a stone of a gravelly field
   I found a shape of a woman.
The woman was resting herself
   from her laborious life.
Our mother
just like our mother.
Oh, no. She's like my own mother.

Some scabs formed over her wounds
   when she got hurt or collapsed.
Enduring the painful time
   and the itching time as well,
has she made
her dream come true
over vibration and wavelength?

Without stopping her work
   she has lived a very busy life.
Putting down her life on a small chair
   somewhere in the market place,
the woman
looks to say something
but shows some hesitation.

「오세암 이야기」 풍도, 24×33×15cm

오세암 이야기

낮밤을 손 모으고 관세음보살 염불하니
젖도 주고 안아 주고 같이 놀아 주었다고
관음암 눈 속에 묻혀 한겨울을 난 길손이

별들이 스쳐가고 은하 씻긴 자리 아래
밤마다 관음봉을 내려오신 분이 있어
문 열자 그윽한 향기, 목탁소리 가득했다

어머니 부름소리 보살님은 새겨들어
엄동의 눈바람도 가만가만 다스렸나
관세음 어머니 품 속 따스하고 올올하다

A Story of Oseam Temple

Gilson* prayed to Amitabha
   with his hands clasped day and night,
which made someone give him milk,
   hug him and play with him.
So the boy spent the midwinter
   in snow at Kwanumam Temple.

Under the passing stars
   and the flowing Milky Way
a Merciful Being came down
   from Mt. Kwanum every night.
When the boy opened the door,
   there's a good smell and wood-block sounds.

The Buddhist Goddess listened
    to the little boy call his mother,
and made a snowy wind blow calmly
    though it was the coldest winter.
The Goddess of Mercy had
    Mom's warm and sweet bosom.

* Gilson : the name of a boy, aged 5, who left home to look for his mother.

「사랑 앞에」 병곡, 16×15×9cm

사랑 앞에

서동

마 캐어 등에 메고 국경 땅을 통과하며
산 넘고 물을 건너 그대 찾아 가는 날은
두 발이 뜬구름처럼 가볍기만 하였으랴

선화

얼굴 한 번 본 적 없는 짝사랑 이더라도
땅 하늘 구분 없이 눈꽃처럼 피는 눈물
이렇게 만나는 것이 그대와 나 운명이라면

In Front of Love

Seodong [1]

On the day I passed the border
   with some grubbed hemps on my back
and went off to meet you
   over mountains and across streams,
how my feet were not so light
   as a floating and drifting cloud.

Seonhwa[2]

I had never met you before.
    It might be just your one-sided love.
But tears came to gush out my eyes
    like flowers to heaven and earth.
It must be the fate of you and me
    that we should meet in this way.

---

1. Seodong : the name of King Muwang(the 30th King of the Baekje Dynasty) when he was young.
2. Seonhwa : a princess of the Sylla Dynasty. She got married to King Muwang.

「심포리 기찻길」 풍도, 10×12×4cm

심포리 기찻길

기찻길 아스라이
한 굽이씩 돌 때마다

아카시아 꽃내음이
그날처럼 향기롭다

아버지
뒷모습 같은
휘굽어진 고향 철길

돌이끼 곱게 갈아
손톱 끝에 물들이고

새로 깔린 자갈밭을
좋아라, 뛰어가면

지금도
내 이름 부르며
아버지가 서 계실까

Shimpori Railroad

Whenever I turn the bends
of the railroad tracks one by one,

the fragrance of acacia
is as good as it was.

The bent tracks
of my native place
remind me of my father's back.

After I dye my nails pretty
with well-mashed stone moss,

if I run to my father with joy
passing the newly gravelly field,

can I see
him standing there
calling my name as before?

「선덕의 외출」 동해, 26×19×9cm

선덕의 외출

신라적 여왕님이 돌 속에 납시었다
가을빛도 무색한 날 궁궐을 돌아 나와
사뿐히 가시는 길이 그 어딘가, 궁금하다

궁녀들도 다소곳이 뒤따른 저 모양새
자그마한 저 돌 속에 언제부터 드시었나
시간이 멈춰선 여기 그 옛날이 살아 있다

사모하는 맘이 깊어 수척해진 지귀에게
손목의 팔찌 풀어 가슴팍에 얹어줄 때
주름진 옷자락 사이 금빛햇살 쏟아졌다

Queen Seondeok's[1] Outing

A queen of the Sylla Dynasty
   appeared onto this stone.
On the day of bright autumn tints
   she came out of her palace.
I wonder where she's going now
   lightly with her soft steps.

Some court ladies accompany her
   on the walk obediently.
Since when has she been there
   on the very smallish stone?
Time has stopped right here at this place;
   the ancient times seem to revive.

When Jigui[2] got haggard
  from his lovesickness toward her,
she took off her own bracelet
  and put it on his chest.
At that time the sun shed golden beams
  through the folds of her dress.

1. Queen Seondeok(? - A.D. 647) : the 27th monarch of the Sylla Dynasty (B.C. 57~A.D. 935)
2. Jigui : a lowly young man who fell in love at first sight when he saw Queen Seondeok. But his love was one-sided.

「아침, 정동진」동해, 10×8×4.5cm

아침, 정동진

왈칵,
바다를 열자
찬바람이 뺨을 갈긴다
군마가 달려간 자리
뽀오얗게 이는 포말
언덕 위 썬크루즈가 그 속으로 빠져든다

천지의 자궁문이
조심스레 열린다
신의 손이 밀어 올리는 저 싱그런 햇덩이!
뚝, 뚝, 뚝
듣는 황금물
온 바다가 환하다

청춘이
한 걸음도
물러서지 않는 자리
너와 나 달려가야 할 붉은 이유 거기 두고
신년호 닻을 올린다
이제 다시 시작이다

The Morning of Jeongdongjin[1]

With a rush I open the sea;
thereon a cold wind slaps my cheeks.
Where warhorse-like waves run away,
milky white sea bubbles form.
The Suncruise[2] on the hill over there
seems to fall into the bubbles.

The womb of heaven and earth
is opening warily.
The hand of the Supreme Being
pushes up the sweet fresh sun!
Now behold the dripping golden water.
The whole sea is brightening.

Young boys and girls staying there
never take even one step backward.
Along with the hot reason
why you and I must run,
New Year's Boat pulls up its anchor;
now is the time to start again.

1. Jeongdongjin : a seaside town in Kangwon Province, Korea. It is famous for its New Year's Sunrise Festival.
2. The Suncruise : a famous hillside hotel in Jeongdongjin. Its shape is a big cruise ship.

「부표를 읽다」 삼섬, 13×24×8cm

부표를 읽다
— 제주 해녀

바다와 첫 상견례 후 거처를 옮겼는지
물결의 갈기 속을 제 집처럼 드나들며
등줄기 꼿꼿이 세워 숨비소리 뱉는다

낡고 헌 망사리만큼 한 생도 기우뚱한
햇살 잘게 부서지는 물속을 텃밭 삼아
수평선 그쯤에 걸린 이마를 씻는 나날

손아귀에 움켜진 게 목숨 같은 것이어서
노을도 한 번씩은 붉디붉게 울어줄 때
등 푸른 고등어같이 잠녀들이 떠 있다

Reading the Buoy
— Jeju's female divers

After the first meeting with the sea
   the divers seem to have moved.
Thinking of a mane of waves as their home,
   they come into and go out of waves.
Erecting their back bones, they breathe out
   as coming out of the sea.

Their lives are as shaky
   as their own worn-out net bags.
The women deem shiny underwater
   their vegetable garden.
Day by day they wash their forehead
   somewhere on the horizon.

The things, which they have in their hands,
  are as precious as their own life.
When the setting sun cries
  ruddily once in a while,
the divers are floating on the water
  just like green-back mackerels.

「안개에 젖어」 동해, 15×22×7cm

안개에 젖어

생애의 선택 집중
그 속을 질주하다

질주에 놓쳐버린
갈림길의 분기점

분기점
그 자리마다
선연하게 길이 핀다

길이 피자 짙은 안개
푸른 산을 뜸들이고

뜸이 오른 산중턱에
수증기가 퍼질 무렵

퍼져서
감싸인 산허리
젖은 길이 봉긋하다

Being Wet in the Mist

Focusing on my selection of life
I've taken a scamper in the life.

But I used to miss the scamper
at the junction of a forked road.

Then right there
at every junction
I've found another road clearly.

When a road comes to be seen,
a thick haze hangs over the green hills.

By the time vapors spread out
to the misty mountainsides,

a wet road
looks to jut forward
from the hillsides veiled in mist.

「모래울음을 찾아」 동해, 8×8×5cm

모래울음을 찾아

돈황 명사산鳴沙山에
모여 사는 바람 있다

잔양殘陽이 능선 위로
저미듯 스며들 때

발자국 남기지 않는
길목을 따라 간다

아랫녘은 푹푹 빠져
발목이 다 잠겨도

바람이 다져 놓은
언덕으로 오를수록

단단한 울음의 뼈가
문양으로 드러난다

In Search of the Sand Crying

On Mingsha Shan[1] of Dunhuang[2]
some winds live together.

When the setting sun sinks down
to the ridge of a sand dune,

we all walk along a path,
which doesn't leave our footsteps.

At the foot of every dune
our feet fall into sands.

But as we go higher up the dunes,
which some winds have trodden down,

the hard bones caused by its crying
appear in certain patterns.

1. Mingsha Shan : Dunes of the Crying Sands in Dunhuang city, China
2. Dunhuang : an oasis city in China

제2부

꽃밤

The Flowering Night

「꽃밤」 을미도, 17×15×8cm

꽃밤

산수유 핀 등성이
어둠을 밀고 있다

누군가 달아 놓은
매화 꽃등 두엇 아래

첼로를 연주하는가,
그대를 알 듯 말 듯

The Flowering Night

The ridge, where cornel dogwoods bloom,
is pushing the darkness away.

Under a few *ume** blossoms
like a lamp which someone hung,

do you play the cello by chance?
I may or may not know you.

* ume : a Japanese apricot tree

「농악놀이」 을미도, 20×14×9cm

농악놀이

한 무리 농악대가 흥에 겨운 장마당에
기수들과 잡이들이, 춤을 추는 잡색까지
풍년가 굿거리장단 열두 발 상모 돈다

풍년 기원 오체투지 온 마을 불 밝히고
하늘을 열어 젖혀 그 뜻을 듣게 하니
땅속도 화합하듯이 울림으로 번져 간다

The Play of a Farm Band

A farm band plays together
   at the festive marketplace.
Flagmen, drummers and dancers play
   to the traditional Gutgeory rhythm
of a song for good harvest
   along with 12-ling Sangmo dancers.

With a prayer for good harvest,
   they play hard from top to toe.
With the village brightly lit up,
   they open the sky to make it listen.
In accord is the underground,
   and its resonance spreads all over.

「누가 오시나」 풍도, 17×28×14cm

누가 오시나

가슴엔
꿈주머니
허파처럼 달고 있다

먼 곳을 바라보는
소녀의 표정 속에

단정한 단발머리가
한쪽으로 기운다

Who's Gonna Come

On her chest
the girl has
a dream pocket like her lungs.

She looks as if she sees
somewhere far away.

To one side her clear-cut bobbed hair
is being more and more tilted .

「달밤」 을미도, 10×8×4cm

달밤

구름 속을 나온 달이
저 환한 보름달이

가을 하늘 가운데를
둥두렷 밝혀든다

지상은
단풍빛 축제
가을 적막 다 적시고

A Moonlight Night

The moon which came out of clouds -
the extremely bright full moon

makes the center of the autumn sky
explicitly brighter than ever.

The ground holds
a scarlet festival
in the autumn silence.

「꽃, 그 순간」 병곡, 9×16×9cm

꽃, 그 순간

하늘의 벅찬 숨결
그대로 땅이 받아

홀로된 꽃대궁도
꽃씨를 받아 둔다

순간은 모두 꽃이다
네 남루도 그렇다

A Flower, at the Momentt

The formidable breathing of the sky
the earth takes over, as it is.

Even the stalk, which's left alone,
sets aside its flower seeds.

The moment in all is a flower.
So are your tattered clothes.

「그리고, 별」 동해, 10×10×5cm

그리고, 별

내 마음
활주로에
너는 뜨고 내리는가

시간의
하얀 촉루
밤하늘을 닦는 동안

가슴엔
스멀거리는
별이 하나 돋았다

And, the Star

Do you dare
to take off and land on
on the runway of my heart?

During the time
when the white droppings
of time polished well a night sky,

in my heart
a star came up
creepy and crawly.

「가을 뎃생」 풍도, 11×7×6.5cm

가을 뎃생

바람도 만취인가
갈밭길이 술렁인다

높을 대로 높은 하늘
저도 잠시 취하는지

흰 구름 몇 송이 뜯어
제멋대로 널어놨다

An Autumn Sketch

Is the wind also blind drunk?
The field of reeds is restless.

The lofty high sky, too,
looks to be drunk for a while.

The sky picked a few of white clouds
and spread them out as it pleased.

「고목」동해, 26×40×17cm

고목

해질녘 비쳐오는
황금빛 시간 사이

늠름하게 어깨 겨눈
소나무를 보았는가

온 시름 내려놓고 가는
시와 꿈 사이
빛과 잠 사이

An Aged Tree

Between the times of golden light
at the dusk of an evening,

have you seen gallant pine trees
standing shoulder to shoulder

without grief
between poems and dreams
between lights and sleeps?

「강론하는 교황님」 풍도, 27×24×13cm

강론하는 교황님

늘어뜨린 사제복에
오롯이 깃든 평화

흩어진 마음자리
한 곳에 모으신다

우러러
보는 눈길에
등대인가, 저 불빛!

The Preaching Pope

There's peace hanging wholly
onto the pope's drooping robe.

He attracts scattered minds
into only one place.

To the people
who look up to him,
his light may be a light house!

「과묵」삼천포, 8×14×6cm

과묵

높고 깊은 생각 있어
입술에 힘이 간다

저, 도인
한 말씀 할 듯
뭐라고 꾸짖을 듯

끝내는 말문 닫은 입
감아 외려 형형한 눈빛

Reticence

His high and deep thinking
makes his lips firm and tight.

The Taoist
seems to preach
a sermon or reproach me.

But rather he keeps silence;
I feel a flash from his closed eyes.

「난송이 두엇」 삼섬, 20×21×18cm

난 송이 두엇

꽃샘잎샘 다 넘어온
거룩한 봄의 얼굴

둥근 그 향 받쳐 드는
꽃대들의 안부인가

양각된 시간이 핀다,
봄향香 가득 쟁여 있다

A Few Orchid Flowers

These holy faces of spring
got over the cold of early spring.

Do the faces show the well-being
of the flower stalks holding its scent?

Embossed time comes out of it,
filled with the fragrance of spring.

「저 길을 따라서」 삼섬, 16×16×7cm

저 길을 따라서

저 길을
따
 라
  서
가을이
오고 있다

저 길을
따
 라
  서
가을이
가고 있다

오가는
길
 은
  하
   나
    다
시간들이
다를 뿐

Along the Way

Along the
w
  a
    y
autumn
is coming.

Along the
w
  a
    y
autumn
is going.

But the way
i
  s
    o
      n
        e.
Only the times
are different.

제3부
부부
Husband and Wife

「부부」을미도, 9×16×6cm(우)
을미도, 9×15×6cm(좌)

부부

우리 함께
가는 길은
산길 들길 모래밭길

때로는 눈비 오고
된바람에 길 막혀도

서로 안
머무는 눈길
봄볕으로 감싼 우리

Husband and Wife

The way we two go
is a mountain path,
a field path, or a sand path.

Sometimes we meet snow or rain,
and a gail prevents our way.

But we wrap
ourselves in the spring sunshine
with our knowing and loving glance.

「돌꽃, 진달래」 풍도, 8×13×6cm

돌꽃, 진달래

사월이 아니라도
꽃내음이 가득하다

한 아름 꽃술 아래
흐르는 별무더기

청록빛
줄기 사이로
지지 않는 봄 얼굴

Stone Blossoms, Azalea

Though it is not April yet,
the air is laden with their scent.

A cluster of stars glitter
under an armful of stamens.

The spring face
still looks young and fresh,
between bluish green stems.

「담금질」을미도, 20×36×20cm

담금질

불가능을 가능하게 부정을 긍정으로
허기도 포만도 아닌 몇 번의 식탐까지
생각을 한 바퀴 돌려 제자리에 놓는다

그렇게 똬리 틀고 참선에 든 늦은 오후
우려낸 진국으로 뽀얗게 피는 그것
수굿이 솟아오르는 시마詩魔 마저 고아본다

Tempering

I make the impossible possible,
   and make the negative positive.
Neither hunger nor satiety,
   I feel gluttony a few times.
Upon this I set it all right
   after a round of thoughts.

In the late afternoon I sit
   and practice Zen meditation.
To get the milky white essence
   of the undiluted liquor,
modestly I expect to get
   the siren call of poetry.

「둥근 꽃」 을미도, 12×10×6cm

둥근 꽃

밤새 내 곁에서
뒤채던 물안개가

웅크린 어둠 몰며
환하게 문을 연다

목덜미 붉어오는 아침
꽃잎마다 해가 뜬다

The Round Flower

The water mist, turning and
tossing near me all night long,

pushes away crouching darkness
and opens a door with brightness.

The sun rises to shine every petal,
in the morning dyeing my nape red.

「따스한 입맞춤」 병곡, 6.5×7×3.8cm

따스한 입맞춤

바람 살짝 스치듯이
네가 가만 다가온다

오래 전 안부 묻듯
입김으로 건네는 말

아늑한
봄날의 풀밭
기린 한 쌍 한 몸이다

A Warm Kiss

You come closer and closer
calmly as if a breeze grazes me.

You say with puffs of your breath
as if to ask how I've been.

On the grass
of a mild spring day
a couple of giraffes are one body.

「때때로」풍도, 8.5×15×8cm

때때로

마음이 외로울 땐
큰 나무 곁에 선다

무수한 가지와 잎
흔들리고 흔들리며

안으로
감는 나이테
나의 사랑, 나의 길

Once in a While

When I feel melancholy
I stand by a tall tree.

Its numerous branches and leaves
swing and sway hither and thither.

And inward
its annual ring grows.
It's my love and my way.

「말문을 닫다」 길산도, 19×28×8cm(좌)
을미도, 14×21×10cm(우)

말문을 닫다
— 이심전심

부처님이 묻지 않아도
가섭은 알았다는 듯

다소곳이 모은 손과
수굿하게 숙인 고개

말없이 생각은 만 리,
마른 가슴 꽃이 피네

Saying No More
— The Communion of Heart with Heart

Though Buddha didn't ask him at all,
Gaseop* seemed to know Buddha's mind.

Gaseop put his hands together,
with his head gently drooped.

Silently he was deep in thought;
then his dry heart came into bloom.

* Gaseop : one of Buddha's ten disciples

「매화향기 바람에 날리고」 풍도, 6×10×2.5cm

매화 향기 바람에 날리고

이 봄 다시 피, 겠, 어, 요
그대 깊은 가슴속에

뜨거웠던 눈맞춤의
설레었던 그, 날, 처, 럼

하아얀 향기 날리며
봄날 가득 메울래요

The Fragrance of Ume Flowers Whirled by the Wind

This spring again I'LL BURST OUT
into blossom in your deep heart.

JUST LIKE THE DAY of a throbbing heart
after exchanging our hot glances,

I will fill up the days of spring
with nice and white fragrance.

「불국토」길산도, 8×11×5cm

불국토

그래,
꼭 너처럼
이 가을에 나 취하네

새빨갛게 타더니만
샛노랗게 까무라쳐

불콰한 절집의 얼굴
덩그러니 이 몸 한 채

The Buddha's Land

Yes, really
just like you,
I get tipsy this autumn.

I'm aflame with red tints
and then swoon with yellow tints.

I stay here
with the face of the temple
which puts on autumnal tints.

「비밀」신안, 12×13×10cm

비밀

나 어릴 적 저 물건을
이제와 다시 본다

할머니가 숨겨놓던
꿀단지 아니었나

열 순갈 퍼먹었어도
시침 뚝 떼고 방긋

Secrecy

Now I see again the thing
which I saw in my childhood.

It's like the honey pot
which my grandma used to hide.

With a smile I pretended not to eat,
though I ate ten spoonfuls of honey.

「천불동에 무릎 꿇고」 남한강, 14×24×9cm

천불동에 무릎 꿇고
― 돈황 막고굴

지평선은 가이없고 푸나무도 없는 이 곳
혜초가 더듬어 간 사막의 열기 속에
천 번을 꼽는 손가락 소원마다 꽃을 단다

앉고 서고 모로 누운 부처님 납의納衣 그늘
어쭙잖은 내 속말을 가려 덮어 주시는지
보일 듯 보이지 않게 눈을 뜨고 계시네

Kneeling at Qianfodong[1]
― Mogao[2] Caves in Dunhuang[3]

The horizon is limitless
  and there are no grasses and trees here.
In the heat of the desert
  where Hyecho[4] groped his way,
in blossom comes every wish,
  with finger-counting a thousand times.

Buddha, who sits, stands and lies
  on his side, looks to hide
some of my silly private talks
  under the shade of his robe,
for Buddha is slightly open-eyed
  visibly or invisibly.

1. Qianfodong (meaning "Thousand Buddha Caves"): a stone cave temple in Dunhuang City, China
2. Mogao: another name of Qianfodong
3. Dunhuang: an oasis city in China
4. Hyecho (704-787): a Buddhist monk of the Sylla Dynasty (B.C. 57 ~ A.D. 935). He traveled from Korea to India via China.

제4부
웃음 다이어트
A Laughter Diet

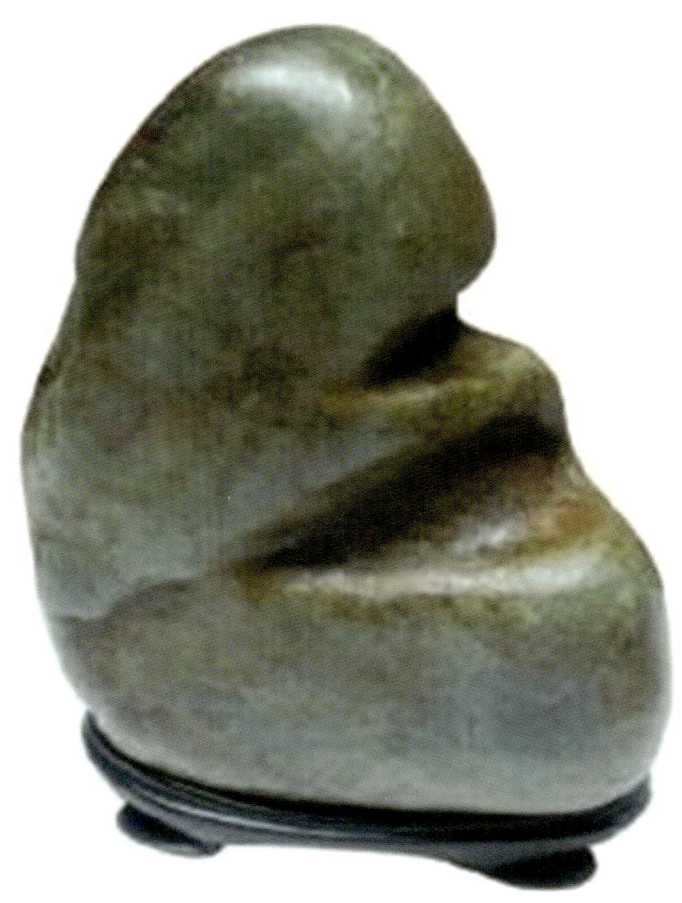

「웃음 다이어트」 삼섬, 22×32×12cm

웃음 다이어트

오관이 짜릿하게
팝콘처럼 뻥, 터지는

바쁜 걸음 멈춰놓고
가벼이 건너시라

군살은 다 빠진 웃음,
구김 없는 저 파안!

A Laughter Diet

You'll get thrills in your five senses
and burst into laughter like popcorns.

So stop your hurried steps
and go over with light steps.

The laughter makes your flab be gone.
See that free and broad smile.

「수양버들」풍도, 11×14×7cm

수양버들

낭창낭창 휘감기는
그대의 머릿결처럼

아침 햇살 끌어 당겨
풀어 놓은 봄의 얼굴

세류細流의
순결한 품 속
안겨드는 바람 좀 봐

A Willow Tree

Just like your good and soft hair
pliantly entwined around,

drawing the morning sunlight,
the tree spreads the face of spring.

See the wind
nestling in the pure breast
of the very small rivulet.

「쉼표」 삼섬, 10×15×10cm

쉼표

물만 먹고 자랐어도
남부럽지 않은 키에

늘씬한 허리 펴고
생각에 잠겨 있다

아는 게
많아질수록
고개 들지 않노라고

A Comma

Eating only water, it's grown up,
but it's as tall as it doesn't envy any.

With its slim waist straightened up,
it indulges in some thought.

It may think;
'as I get to know more,
I will not raise my head.'

「신화」동해, 23×24×12cm

신화

민무늬 토기 가득 마늘과 쑥을 담아
모성으로 거듭났던 전생의 웅녀 모습
털빛도 눈처럼 고운 백곰이 납시었다

열여덟 환히 꽃 핀 아가씨 첫걸음이
눈 감고도 살필 듯이 다소곳 들어올린
한반도 푸른 기상이 핏줄처럼 번지다

A Myth

Filling a no-pattern earthen pot
   with garlics and green mugworts,
the Bear Girl was born again
   with her maternal love.
The lovely white bear came to us,
   wearing a sweet snow-white fur coat.

The 18-year-old lady in her bloom
   takes her first step gently,
as if to look after Korea,
   even with her eyes closed.
Thereupon Korean green spirit
   spreads out like blood vessels.

「십일월 생각」 삼섬, 30×22×12cm

십일월 생각

가을의 등줄기로
단풍이 타고 있다

잘근잘근 밟히며 온
삶의 질긴 근육들이

물들다
물들다 못해
지친 날을 쏟는다

A November Thought

Scarlet-tinged leaves are seated
on the backbone of autumn.

The tough muscles of their life,
which have been trampled down,

are dyed thick
and dyed deeply, resulting
in spitting out their tiring days.

「어부바」 을미도, 18×23×9cm

어부바

칭얼대는 나를 업고
마실 가며 불러주던

"알캉 달캉 우리 애기"
귓가에 들리는 듯

지금도
한밤중 깨면
그립다, 그 따스한 등

Pickaback

When I grizzled, Mom would piggyback
me to the village to have fun,

chanting "*Alkang dalkang*, my baby."
The chant still falls on my ear.

To this day
when I awake at midnight
I yearn much after her warm back.

「어유도」동해, 26×40×17cm

어유도 魚遊圖

수초와 수초 사이
물비늘 일으키며

유연한 긴 꼬리가
낮과 밤을 이어 준다

하늘도
흥을 돋우며
흰 구름 풀어낸다

A Fish-playing Painting

Ruffling the water surface
between some green water weeds,

flexible long slim tails
connect daytime and nighttime.

The sky, too,
strews white cotton clouds,
adding to the mirth of it.

「장독」동해, 10×13×10cm

장독대

한겨울 장독대에 내리는 눈 고요한데
백석의 그림자가 차고 희게 설핏하다
어디서 당나귀 울음 어둠 뚫고 달려올 듯

지금 막 배달돼 온 설국의 엽서 한 장
자작나무 숲 사이로 따라 온 바람하고
온밤 내 흰 눈을 쓴 채 동안거에 드시나

A Soy-jar Terrace

It is snowing now in peace
   on the soy-jar terrace in midwinter.
The shadow of the poet Baek Seok
   is faintly felt cold and white.
The hee-haw of a donkey seems
   to be heard somewhere through the dark.

A postcard has just been delivered
   somewhere from a snow country.
Along with a wind blowing
   out of a white birch forest,
the postcard may do winter meditation,
   covered with white snow all night long.

「절규」 풍도, 15×20×11cm

절규

입을 한껏 벌린 채로
뭐라고 뱉어내는

또 뭐라고 애원하는
그대는 뭉크인가

귀 씻고
나도 들어가
억울한 일 말해볼까

The Scream

With your mouth wide open
you seem to grumble about something.

Or else you may implore something.
Are you possibly Munch*?

May I say
my unfair treatment in it
after I clean my ears?

* Munch(1863~1944) : Edvard Munch. A Norwegian painter.

「주목 앞에서」동해, 22×22×12cm

주목 앞에서

살아서 이루고픈 꿈이 무엇이길래
이미 죽은 가지 끝이 뭐라고 말을 한다
그 말을 받아쓰느라 바람결이 움찔한다

내 생의 발자국에 우기가 지나간다
사막을 건너느라 부르튼 시간의 발
죽어도 여기 보란 듯, 그 맨발을 내보인다

In Front of a Yew Tree

While this tree was alive,
  I wonder what its dream was.
The tips of the branches,
  which are already dead, say something.
Writing down what the tips are saying,
  a breeze twists and turns staggering.

On the footprints of my life,
  the rainy season passes.
My feet have been blistered
  from crossing the desert of life.
I put forth my blistered bare feet,
  as if to surely show them off.

「주상절리」 풍도, 11×10×5cm

주상절리

어깨를
들썩이며
울컥울컥 쏟아내던

접동새 울음 같은
진달랫빛 수석 한 점

마음껏
울지 못하고
잠이 든 절벽처럼

A Columnar Joint

Twitching
its shoulders
and having a fit of crying,

an azalea-hued viewing stone
is just like a screech owl.

It's a cliff
which falls asleep,
not having its cry out.

「폭포와 시」동해, 15×13×7cm

폭포와 시

단 한 번 직활강으로
내려 뛰는 저 단애

고생대 불던 바람
회오리로 찾아들어

물보라 무지개 건넌다
두 눈이 멀지라도

내 몸의 관절마다
푸른 별이 돋는다

그 몸속 지층 어디
울렁이는 어지럼증

시 앞에 고꾸라진 채
목숨 놓을 지라도

The Waterfall and Poems

By making a schuss just once
the precipitous cliff jumps down.

The Paleozoic wind
visits here as a whirlwind.

The rainbow of its splash it crosses,
though its eyes become blinded.

From every joint of my body
green stars have come out.

A certain layer in my body
feels nauseant vertigo.

But I'll write at the risk of my life
though I topple down in front of poems.

제5부
첫눈 오는 날
The Day of the First Snow

「첫눈 오는 날」풍도, 7×8×4cm

첫눈 오는 날

첫눈 오면
달려가리
그대에게 달려가리

펄펄펄
온몸 위로
첫눈 내려 쌓일 동안

첩첩첩
온 마음 위로
그대 사랑 쌓으리

The Day of the First Snow

On the day
of the first snow
I'll run, I'll run to thee.

As the snow
falls thick to pile
upon all over my body,

thy love piles
upon my mind thick
layer upon layer.

「촛대바위」 가덕도, 19×15×7cm

촛대 바위

애국가를 배경으로
우리가 손 모을 때

누구의 간절함이
저렇듯 솟아올라

비바람
폭풍 속에도
맑고 밝게 닦이는가

A Candlestick-shaped Rock

When we put our hands together
listening to our national anthem,

whose aspiration on earth
soars so high into the sky,

burnishing
clearly and brightly
even in the rainstorm?

「풍악산을 건너다」 동해, 29×21×13cm

풍악산을 건너다

말로는 형용 못할
돌빛으로 앉은 천 년

수 만 번을 끌어안아
다듬어 낸 모서리들

파도가
왔다간 흔적
단풍물도 환하다

Crossing Mt. Pungak

For a thousand years it has sat there,
stone-colored beyond description.

Its jags, which has been carved
by tens of thousands of hugs,

bear the marks of splashing waves.
Bright is the red-tinged water, too.

「모과」 을미도, 14×24×15cm

모과

오래 참고 견디느라
단단해진 속살에는

농축된 가을향이
하마 터질듯하다

부르면
달려와 줄 너
다순 눈길 그윽하다

A Quince

The flesh bore and forbore for long,
becoming hard and solid.

The condensed fruit aroma
of autumn is ready to burst.

When you're called
you'll come for certain.
So deep are your warm eyes.

「해빙기」병곡, 15×22×11cm

해빙기

쩌-엉쩡
금이 간다
오랜 날 기다림 끝

아슴아슴
눈을 뜨는
갯버들 솜털의 봄

햇살에
감전된 고요
볼그족족 꽃눈 뜬다

The Thawing Season

With a crack
the ice breaks.
Our long waiting is over.

It's the spring
of the pussy willow fluff
which opens its drowsy eyes.

By sunshine
silence is shocked
and flowers bloom ruddily.

「해수관음보살」 삼섬, 7.5×9×4cm

해수관음보살

어둠의 골짜기를
홀로 밝혀 섰습니다

당신이 켜든 촛불
세상 환히 받쳐 들자

하늘도 허리를 굽혀
길 하나를 냅니다

The Buddhist Goddess Facing the Sea

You are standing alone,
brightening a dark valley.

As the candlelight in your hand
holds up the world with brightness,

the heaven also bends itself
and provides a new road for you.

「홍매」 동해, 8.5×8.5×6cm

홍매

달빛 한 사발을
누가 건져 올리는가

차르르르
물소리가
봄밤을 다 적신다

짧아도
너무 짧았던
그 밤에 스친,
눈빛

Red Apricot Blossoms

I wonder who's picking up
a bowl of the moonlight.

Gushhh gusssh.
The sound of water
drenches a spring night.

On the night,
which's short,
much too short,
their look flits through my mind.

「황산벌에서」 삼섬, 30×25×18cm

황산벌에서

결사대 오천을 끌고 계백이 나가신다

결연하게 부릅뜬 눈 갈기 세운 깃발들

저 기백 푸른 칼날이 부러져도 다시 선다

At the Hwangsan Plain

General Kyeback goes to war,
 with a forlorn hope of 5000 men,

Their eyes glare with a firm purpose
 and their flags are fluttering.

The spirit will be restored again,
 though their sharp swords are broken.

「휘파람」 삼섬, 18×17×8cm

휘파람

잿가루 듬뿍 묻혀
놋그릇을 닦아내듯
햇가루 가득 묻혀
묵은 봄을 닦는다
던져둔 화두를 찾아
입을 한껏 모으는 봄

혈류를 막고 있던
더딘 꿈의 알갱이들
일렁이는 기운으로
피돌기가 한창이다
그 누가 날 벼리는가
저 환한 꽃 길 천 리

Whistle

As if to polish up brassware
with plenty of ash powder,
I wipe out the old spring
with plenty of the sunshine.
In search of the talking subject,
I pucker up my mouth this spring.

The tardy grains of my dream
once prevented my blood stream.
But now thanks to the bobbing spirit,
my blood circulation goes well.
Who urges me to the bright road -
a thousand miles of a flower road?

「흑룡이 날으샤」 을미도, 25×22×13cm

흑룡이 날으샤

여의주를 막 받아 문
흑룡 한 마리가

꽃구름 헤쳐 가며
제 갈 길 바라본다

그 오래
꿈꾸어 오던
천국의 문, 열린다

A Black Dragon Flies

With a big round glass in its mouth,
a gigantic black dragon

takes a look at its own way,
shoving aside a flower of clouds.

Now the door
of Heaven opens,
which's been dreamed for a long time

「타클라마칸 사막」 을미도, 9×8×4cm

타클라마칸 사막

한 때는 물이 흘렀을
건천을 지나가며

내 생도 지고 가는
목마른 낙타 등에

사막을 가로질러온
낮달 저만 드높다

이곡주 한 모금에
길은 자꾸 늘어지고

죽비로 치는 햇살
온 몸으로 견뎌내며

시간을 되감아간다
모랫바람 비단길

The Taklamakan Desert

I pass by the dry stream
where there used to be water.

On the back of the thirsty camel
I put my hard life, too.

The day moon, having crossed the desert,
rises over there high in the sky.

Just a sip of Chinese liquor
makes our way longer and longer.

Enduring the strong sunlight,
which seems to lash with a bamboo stick,

we go now, rewinding the time
in the sandy wind of the Silk Road.

「대흥사 부처님께」 삼섬, 13×20×13cm

대흥사 부처님께

그 골짜기 동백 숲에
사시사철 바람 불어

　가끔은 헝클린 머릿결도 빗겨주고 옷자락, 마음자락 펄럭여 주기도 했지 손가락 가락 사이에도 묻어나던 물향기, 구름향기, 진솔향기, 사랑향기 청신암 맑은 약수에 마음을 빠뜨리고 대웅전 부처님께 엎드려 아뢴 말, 철모르는 내 사랑은 피고 피고 또 피는데, 지고 지고 또 지는 님의 마음 어쩌냐고…

천불전
낡은 싸리비가
한겨울을 다 쓸 동안

To Buddha of the Daeheung Temple

A wind blows in all seasons
in a camellia grove of the vale.

Sometimes the wind combed my neglected hair, and my clothes and my heart fluttered in the wind. The sweet smells of water, clouds, pine trees and love were between my fingers. I put my mind in a clear mineral spring near Chungshinam, and said, lying on my face, to Buddha of the main sanctuary of the temple, "My naive love blooms, blooms and blooms, but his mind wanes, wanes and wanes. What should I do."

At the time
an old besom of Chunbuljeon
swept midwinter away.

| 저자 소개 Introduction of the Author |

김민정 金珉延

시조시인. 문학박사(성균관대학교). 1985년 ≪시조문학≫ 창간 25주년 지상백일장 장원등단. 시조집 『나 여기에 눈을 뜨네』, 『지상의 꿈』, 『사랑하고 싶던 날』, 『영동선의 긴 봄날』, 『백악기 붉은 기침』, 『바다열차』, 『모래울음을 찾아』. 수필집 『사람이 그리운 날엔 기차를 타라』. 평설집 『모든 순간은 꽃이다』. 논문집 『현대시조의 고향성』 외 다수 발간. 나래시조문학상, 열린시학상, 한국문협작가상 수상. 현재 한국문인협회 회원, 국제펜한국본부 회원, 한국시조시인협회 이사, 강동문인협회 부회장, 한국여성시조문학회 명예회장, 나래시조시인협회 회장.

Min-Jung Kim

She is a Sijo poetess and received her ph.D. in Korean literature from SungKyunKwan University. She made her literary debut in 1985, when she won the first place in a literary contest, which was held in celebration of the 25 years' existence after the literary magazine *SijoMunhak* was first published. Her sijo poetry collections include *I Open My Eyes Here, An Earthly Dream, The Long Spring Day of Youngdong Line, A Red Cough of the Cretaceous Period, and A Sea Train, In Search of the Sand Crying.* She published her essay collection *Take a Train When You Miss Someone*, her commentary *Every Moment is a Flower*, her paper *On the Meaning of Hometowns Shown in the Modern Sijo Poems*, etc. She received the Narae-Sijo Prize, the Yeollin-sihak Prize and the Korean Writers' Association Prize. Presently she is a member of the Korean Writers' Association, a member of the Korea PEN under the International PEN, a director of the Korea Association of Sijo Poets, a vice president of Kangdong Writers' Association, an honorary president of the Korea Literary Society of Sijo Poetesses, and the president of the Narae Sijo Poets' Association.

| 번역자 소개 Introduction of the Translator |

우형숙禹亨淑

번역가. 시조시인. 맥번역연구소 대표. 숙명여자대학교와 세종대학교(겸임교수)에서 후학양성. 숙명여자대학교 영문학 학사 및 석사. 세종대학교 영문학 박사(번역학 전공). 2013년 변영로 시詩 번역으로 숙명 문학상 수상. 번역 관련 주요 논문「한영韓英 시詩 번역의 결속구조 연구」,「동화 번역을 위한 결속 요소 연구」,「동시 번역법」,「한영 번역 오류 분석」등. 주요 번역서 변영로의『진달래 동산』과『코리언 오딧세이』, 변영태의『한국의 시가詩歌』, 모나 베이커의『라우트리지 번역학 백과사전』(공역).

Hyung-Sook Woo

She is a translator, a sijo poetess, and a representative of Mac Translation Center, and worked as an adjunct professor of Sejong University and a lecturer of Sookmyung Women's University. She received her B.A. & M.A. in English literature at Sookmyung Women's University, and received her ph.D. in translation studies at Sejong University. Her translations of poems by Young-ro Byun were awarded the 2013 Literary Prize of Sookmyung Women's University. Her papers on translation include 'On Cohesion in Korean-English Poetry Translation', 'On Cohesive Features for the Translation of Juvenile Stories', 'On Methods of Translating Children's Verse', etc. Her translated books include *Grove of Azalea* by Young-ro Byun, *Korean Odyssey* by Young-ro Byun, and *Songs from Korea* by Young-tae Byun. She also co-translated *Routledge Encyclopedia of Translation Studies* by Mona Baker.

e-mail : hyungswoo@hanmail.net

고요아침 운문정신 014

누가, 앉아 있다

초　판 1쇄 인쇄일 · 2017년 08월 21일
초　판 1쇄 발행일 · 2017년 08월 30일

지은이 ｜ 김민정
펴낸이 ｜ 노정자
펴낸곳 ｜ 도서출판 고요아침
편　집 ｜ 김남규

출판등록 2002년 8월 1일 제 1-3094호
03678 서울시 서대문구 증가로 29길 12-27 102호
전　화 ｜ 02-302-3194~5
팩　스 ｜ 02-302-3198
E-mail ｜ goyoachim@hanmail.net
홈페이지 ｜ www.goyoachim.com

ISBN 978-89-6039-986-0(04810)

* 책 가격은 뒤표지에 표시되어 있습니다.
* 지은이와 협의에 의해 인지는 생략합니다.
* 잘못된 책은 교환해 드립니다.

ⓒ 김민정, 2017